AF270632

GREEN BAY
PACKERS

KENNY ABDO

Fly!
An Imprint of Abdo Zoom
abdobooks.com

abdobooks.com

Published by Abdo Zoom, a division of ABDO, P.O. Box 398166, Minneapolis, Minnesota 55439. Copyright © 2022 by Abdo Consulting Group, Inc. International copyrights reserved in all countries. No part of this book may be reproduced in any form without written permission from the publisher. Fly!™ is a trademark and logo of Abdo Zoom.

Printed in the United States of America, North Mankato, Minnesota.
052021
092021

Photo Credits: AP Images, iStock, Shutterstock PREMIER
Production Contributors: Kenny Abdo, Jennie Forsberg, Grace Hansen
Design Contributors: Candice Keimig, Neil Klinepier

Library of Congress Control Number: 2020919497

Publisher's Cataloging-in-Publication Data

Names: Abdo, Kenny, author.
Title: Green Bay Packers / by Kenny Abdo
Description: Minneapolis, Minnesota : Abdo Zoom, 2022 | Series: NFL teams |
    Includes online resources and index.
Identifiers: ISBN 9781098224622 (lib. bdg.) | ISBN 9781098225568 (ebook) |
    ISBN 9781098226039 (Read-to-Me ebook)
Subjects: LCSH: Green Bay Packers (Football team)--Juvenile literature. | National
    Football League--Juvenile literature. | Football teams--Juvenile literature. |
    American football--Juvenile literature. | Professional sports--Juvenile literature.
Classification: DDC 796.33264--dc23

TABLE OF CONTENTS

GREEN BAY PACKERS

When it comes to **Super Bowl** wins and NFL championships, the Green Bay Packers are football's big cheese.

The Packers are the only team in the NFL that is owned publicly by its fans. And they work hard for their 360,000 bosses.

KICK OFF

The Packers became a team in 1919. The team was set up by sports editor George Calhoun and former high school star football player Earl "Curly" Lambeau. Lambeau played for the Packers as halfback and was its first head coach.

Lambeau worked for the Indian Packing Company. The company helped pay for the team during its early years. This is where the team name "Packers" came from.

In 1923, the team became a **nonprofit corporation**. Shares of the team were owned by local businessmen. Today, the Packers are still community owned.

By 1936, the Packers had
already won their fourth
NFL title! The team defeated
Boston with a 21-6 victory.

TEAM RECAPS

Green Bay played in the very first **Super Bowl** on January 15, 1967. With Max McGee's seven catches for 138 yards and two touchdowns, the Packers beat the Chiefs 35-10! The next year, they won Super Bowl II against the Oakland Raiders 33-14.

The Packers went to back-to-back **Super Bowls** again in 1997 and 1998. On January 26, 1997, the Packers defeated the Patriots 35-21. The next year, the Broncos beat the Packers in an **upset**.

Quarterback Brett Favre broke the NFL record by throwing his 421st touchdown pass in a victory against the Minnesota Vikings in September of 2007.

The Packers played in their fifth **Super Bowl** in 2011 after Favre had left the team. They beat the Pittsburgh Steelers 31–25.

PACKERS
89
NFL

The Packers finished the 2019 season with a 13-3 record. They went on to win the **division** playoffs against the Seahawks. Left Tackle David Bakhtiari was named an **AP All-Pros**. Five Packers players were selected for the 2020 **Pro Bowl**.

Quarterback Aaron Rodgers was the NFL's leader in passer rating for the 2020 season. The Packers closed out the season with another 13-3 record, placing first in **NFC** North **division**!

Donald Driver played wide receiver for
the Packers for his entire 14-season
career. He had seven 1,000-yard seasons!

Driver also caught a total of 743 passes for 10,137 receiving yards, more than any other Packer.

Brett Favre was named the NFL's **MVP** three times. In 1997, he led the Packers to their third **Super Bowl** win. During his NFL career, Favre broke many passing records and played 297 consecutive games starting at **QB**. Favre was inducted into the Pro Football Hall of Fame in 2016.

Aaron Rodgers was drafted by the Packers in 2005. He has earned many career awards and records. In 2021, he became only the sixth player to be named NFL's **MVP** at least three times!

GLOSSARY

AP All-Pro – an honor given by press organizations to professional NFL players that names the best player at each position during a season.

division – a group of teams who compete against each other for a championship.

MVP – short for "most valuable player," an award given in sports to a player who has performed the best in a game or series.

National Football Conference (NFC) – one of two major conferences of the NFL. Each conference contains 16 teams split into four divisions. The winner of the NFC championship plays the AFC.

nonprofit corporation – a business that is tax-exempt because it provides public benefit and furthers social cause.

Pro Bowl – a game played once a year between two teams comprised of the NFL's all-stars.

quarterback (QB) – the player on the offensive team that directs teammates in their play.

Super Bowl – the NFL championship game, played once a year.

upset – in sports, when a team that is expected to win loses or ties a game against an underdog team.

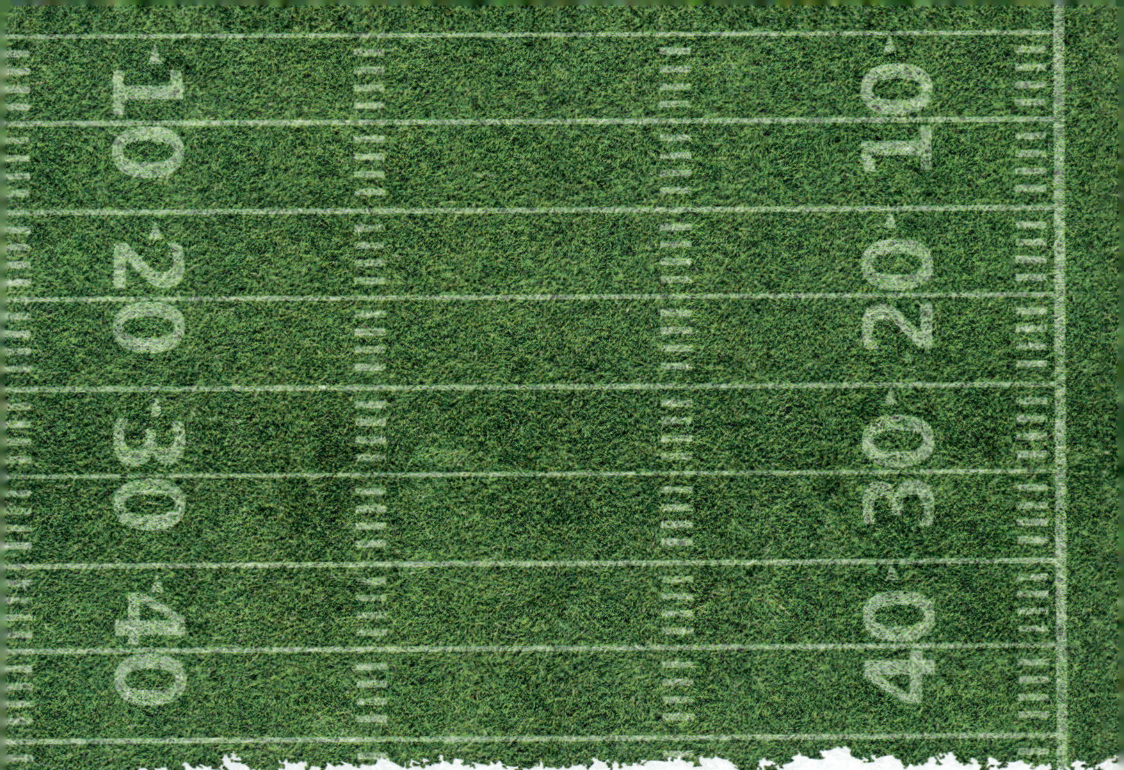

ONLINE RESOURCES

To learn more about the Green Bay Packers, please visit **abdobooklinks.com** or scan this QR code. These links are routinely monitored and updated to provide the most current information available.

INDEX